Reconciliation

RCL Benziger

Allen, Texas

NIHIL OBSTAT
Rev. Msgr. Glenn D. Gardner, J.C.D.
Censor Librorum

IMPRIMATUR
† Most Rev. Charles V. Grahmann
Bishop of Dallas

May 27, 2002

The Nihil Obstat and Imprimatur are official declarations that the material reviewed is free of doctrinal or moral error. No implication is contained therein that those granting the Nihil Obstat and Imprimatur agree with the contents, opinions, or statements expressed.

Send all inquiries to:
RCL Benziger
200 East Bethany Drive
Allen, Texas 75002-3804

Toll Free   877-275-4725
Fax   800-688-8356

Visit us at www.RCLBenziger.com

Printed in the United States of America
by ColorDynamics, Allen, Texas

20451   ISBN 978-0-7829-1007-0 (Child's Book)
20452   ISBN 978-0-7829-1008-7 (Guide)

6 7 8 9 10 11 12 • 13 12 11 10 09 08

ACKNOWLEDGMENTS

Excerpts from the English translation of *Rite of Baptism for Children* © 1969, International Committee on English in the Liturgy, Inc. (ICEL); excerpts from the English translation of *Rite of Penance* © 1974, ICEL. All rights reserved.

Abbreviated as follows: (bkgd) background; (t) top; (b) bottom; (l) left; (r) right; (c) center.

Chapter 1: Page 4 (l), © Margaret Ross/Stock Boston Inc./PictureQuest; 4 (r), © EyeWire; 5, © Reuters NewMedia Inc./Corbis; 8, © Bill & Peggy Wittman.

Chapter 2: Page 12 (l), © Robert Maass/Corbis; 12 (r), © Zefa Visual Media-Germany/Index Stock Imagery/PictureQuest; 13, © Erin Hogan/PhotoDisc; 16, © Donald F. Wristen/RCL; 17, © The Crosiers/Gene Plaisted, OSC.

Chapter 3: Page 20 (l), © Jean Noel Reichel/FPG International; 20 (r), © Jeanene Tiner; 21, © Associated Press/The Merced Sun-Star/Dave Getzschman; 24, © Myrleen Ferguson/PhotoEdit/PictureQuest.

Chapter 4: Page 28 (l), © Jeff Greenberg/Stock Boston Inc./PNI; 28 (r), Rhinestone Productions/SuperStock; 29, © Myrleen Cate/Index Stock Imagery/PictureQuest; 32, © The Crosiers/Gene Plaisted, OSC.

Chapter 5: Page 36 (l), © Mary Kate Denny/PhotoEdit/PictureQuest; 36 (r), © Robin Davies/FPG International; 37, © Kevin R. Morris/Corbis; 40, © The Crosiers/Gene Plaisted, OSC.; 41, © Donald F. Wristen/RCL.

Chapter 6: Page 44 (l), © Tony Freeman/PhotoEdit/PictureQuest; 44 (r), © Don Smetzer/Stone; 45, © Mary Kate Denny/Stone; 48, © The Crosiers/Gene Plaisted, OSC.

Backmatter: Page 52, © Eric Williams/RCL; 53, © Eric Williams/RCL; 54, © Donald F. Wristen/RCL; 55, © Donald F. Wristen/RCL; 56, © Owen Franken/Corbis; 57, © The Crosiers/Gene Plaisted, OSC.; 58, © Sam Martinez/RCL; 59, © Eric Williams/RCL; 60, © The Crosiers/Gene Plaisted, OSC; 61, © James L. Shaffer; 62, © The Crosiers/Gene Plaisted, OSC.; 63, © The Crosiers/Gene Plaisted, OSC.; 66, © The Crosiers/Gene Plaisted, OSC.; 68, © Mary Kate Denny/Stone; 69, © Mary Kate Denny/PhotoEdit/PictureQuest; 70, 80, © The Crosiers/Gene Plaisted, OSC.

Illustration Credits: Jenny Williams/Portfolio Solutions, pp. 6–7, 14–15, 22–23, 30–31, 38–39, 46–47.

Cover Design: Kristy O. Howard

Cover Illustration: Karen Malzeke-McDonald

Dedication

This program is dedicated to
Richard C. Leach
1927–2001
founder and continuing inspiration of RCL
and recipient of the Pro Ecclesia et Pontifice Cross
bestowed by Pope John Paul II in recognition
of outstanding service to the Church.

SACRAMENT PREPARATION DEVELOPMENT TEAM

Developing a sacrament program requires the talents of many gifted people working together as a team. RCL Benziger is proud to acknowledge these dedicated people who contributed to the development of this sacrament preparation program.

Mary Beth Jambor
Writer

Jacquie Jambor
Diane Lampitt
Contributing Writers

Rev. Louis J. Cameli
Theological Advisor

Rev. Robert D. Duggan
Liturgical Advisor

Elaine McCarron, SCN
Catechetical Advisor

Marina A. Herrera
Hispanic Consultant

Lisa Brent
Art and Design Director

Pat Bracken
Kristy O. Howard
Designers

Laura Fremder
Electronic Page Makeup

Jenna Nelson
Production Director

Patricia A. Classick
Ronald C. Lamping
Project Editors

Joseph Crisalli
Demere Henson
Web Site Producers

Ed DeStefano
General Editor

Maryann Nead
President/Publisher

Contents

Chapter 1   We Belong to God 4

Chapter 2   We Follow Jesus 12

Chapter 3   We Listen to the Holy Spirit 20

Chapter 4   We Are Sorry 28

Chapter 5   We Are Forgiven 36

Chapter 6   We Are Peacemakers 44

Celebrating Reconciliation 52

    The Individual Rite for Reconciliation 52

    The Communal Rite for Reconciliation 57

Examination of Conscience 64

The Ten Commandments 65

The Beatitudes 68

The Precepts of the Church 70

My Daily Prayers 71

Glossary 75

Scripture Cards 81

Certificate 85

CHAPTER 1

We Belong to God

Loving God,
you call us each
by our name.

Sharing Together

In the opening prayer you were called by name and blessed with water. What was it like for you?

When are some important times you are called by name?

We are called by the name Christian because we belong to Christ. When we make the sign of the cross, we are telling others we are Christians. Give one example of a time when we make the sign of the cross.

_____

_____

_____

God Loves Us

Jesus told us over and over again that we belong to God. He taught that God knows and calls us by name. Read this story to discover what it means to belong to God.

A shepherd had one hundred sheep. One day the shepherd discovered that one of his sheep was missing. Immediately the shepherd went looking for the one lost sheep.

Soon the shepherd found his lost sheep. The shepherd's heart was filled with joy. He picked up the sheep, put it on his shoulders, and carried it back to the other sheep.

The shepherd was very happy. He shouted to his friends and neighbors, "I have found my lost sheep!"

BASED ON LUKE 15:4–6

FAITH FOCUS

What does it mean to belong to God?

Jesus tells us that God is like a shepherd. What does it mean to call God our shepherd?

TOGETHER AS A FAMILY

Role-play the Bible story. Emphasize that the shepherd never gives up searching for the lost sheep. Help your child to understand that the sheep recognizes the shepherd and comes when he hears the shepherd's voice. Next, discuss responses to the question on this page.

Jesus, the Good Shepherd

WHAT WE SEE AND HEAR

During the celebration of the sacrament of Reconciliation, the priest asks God's blessing on us. He does this by making the sign of the cross and praying, "In the name of the Father, and of the Son, and of the Holy Spirit." This reminds us that there are three Persons in one God—God the Father, God the Son, and God the Holy Spirit.

The Bible story about the shepherd and the lost sheep tells us how much God loves us. Jesus, the Son of God, told another story about a shepherd. It is the story about a good shepherd.

A good shepherd knows each of his sheep by name. When a good shepherd calls one of his sheep by name, the sheep comes to him. A good shepherd cares so much about his sheep that he will give his life to protect his sheep. Jesus told the people that he is a good shepherd. He said,

"I am the good shepherd.
I will give my life for my sheep."

BASED ON JOHN 10:14

Jesus the Good Shepherd gave his life for us. He died on the cross and was raised from the dead to save us from our sins. Jesus' death and resurrection show us how much God loves us.

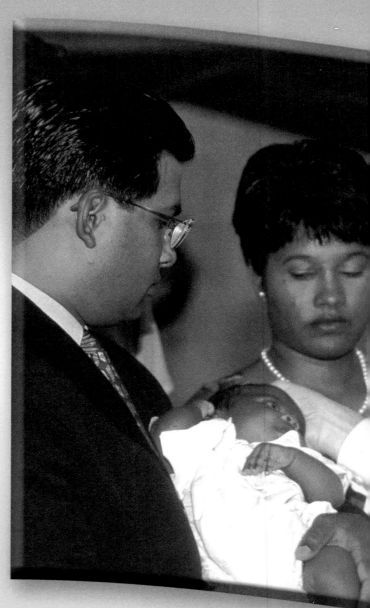

At the beginning of the celebration of Baptism, the priest or deacon calls us by name and says, *(Name),* the Christian community welcomes you with great joy. In its name I claim you for Christ our Savior by the sign of the cross.

He traces a cross on our forehead. Then he invites our parents and godparents to do the same.

The Church celebrates Baptism because Jesus told his followers to baptize people. Baptism joins us to Jesus. We share new life in Christ. We share in Jesus' death and resurrection.

God shares his life with us. We become adopted children of God and members of our church family. Original sin and all other sins are forgiven. We receive the gift of the Holy Spirit. We are given the promise of eternal life.

What happens at Baptism?

TOGETHER AS A FAMILY

Share the story of your child's baptism with your son or daughter. Then discuss responses to the question on this page.

What Difference Does This Make in My Life?

Jesus taught us that we belong to God. God knows and loves each of us. At Baptism God shares his life and love with us. We become adopted children of God. The Holy Spirit helps us to share God's love with others.

Draw or write about how you show God's love for people.

MY FAITH CHOICE

Talk with someone about one thing you will do this week to show God's love for people.

TOGETHER AS A FAMILY

Remembering Together

In this chapter your child learned that we belong to God in a special way. God knows and loves each of us. We become adopted children of God at Baptism. This is a good time for you to talk with your child about Baptism. Include responses to these or similar questions in the discussion:

- Where were you or your child baptized?
- Who baptized you?
- Who are your godparents?
- Who else was at your Baptisms?
- Why were these special days?

Sharing Together

Choose one of the following activities to do together or design a similar activity of your own:

- Look at pictures in your family's photo albums that show each family member's Baptism. Share stories about each Baptism. Tell your child why the name you gave him or her is special and a sign of your love.
- In the Bible story the shepherd looked for the one lost sheep. Think of someone who may be lonely. Name something your family can do for that person.

 Visit the RCL sacraments web site by following the link titled "Sacraments" at www.FaithFirst.com.

Praying Together

Pray this or a similar prayer at family meals or at other family prayer times this week:

> God, our Father,
> we thank you for loving us
> and claiming us as your own.
> Send the Holy Spirit
> to help us live as your children.
> We ask this through Jesus Christ our Lord. Amen.

Getting Ready Together

We begin the celebration of the sacrament of Reconciliation by praying the Sign of the Cross. This is a good time to review with your child the meaning of the Sign of the Cross. The cross is a sign of God's mercy and love for us. At Baptism we are marked with the sign of a cross and claimed for Christ. When we pray the Sign of the Cross and bless ourselves, praying, "In the name of the Father, and of the Son, and of the Holy Spirit. Amen," we remember our Baptism. We remember that we are children of God and that we belong to Christ.

CHAPTER 2

We Follow Jesus

*God of love,
send us the Holy Spirit
to help us follow your word.*

Sharing Together

In the opening prayer we carried the Bible in procession. We gathered together and showed reverence for God's word. What was it like for you to show reverence for the word of God?

How do you show reverence at other times?

As Catholics we show reverence for the Bible, or Sacred Scripture. This means we show our love and respect for the word of God. Give one example of how we show reverence for Sacred Scripture.

_____

_____

_____

The Great Commandment

Sacred Scripture is the holy word of God. Read this Bible story. Discover what Jesus taught about showing our reverence for God, ourselves, and other people.

There was a man who taught people about the commandments. He asked Jesus this question. "Teacher, what is the most important commandment?"

Jesus answered, " 'Love God with all your heart, soul, and mind.' This is the first and greatest commandment. The second commandment is like the first. 'Love others as much as you love yourself.' "

BASED ON MATTHEW 22:34–40

FAITH FOCUS

What does the Great Commandment teach?

Jesus taught about the Great Commandment. What does the Great Commandment teach about showing reverence?

TOGETHER AS A FAMILY

Share the Bible story about the Great Commandment. Discuss responses to the question on this page. This week choose ways that your family members can live the Great Commandment.

Living a Holy Life

FAITH FOCUS

What is the sacrament of Reconciliation?

WHAT WE SEE AND HEAR

The crucifix reminds us that Jesus' dying on the cross shows his love for his Father and for us. We see the crucifix in our church. We also see the crucifix in the reconciliation room. The crucifix reminds us of the way that Jesus lived the Great Commandment.

The Great Commandment tells us that we are to love and respect God, ourselves, and all people. We do what the Great Commandment tells us when we live the Ten Commandments. The first three commandments help us to love and respect God. The last seven commandments help us to love and respect ourselves and others.

God gives every person the gift of a conscience to help us know the commandments. Our conscience helps us to know what is right and what is wrong. It helps us to know what God wants us to do and not to do.

God also gives every person the gift of a free will. This means that we can choose to live or not to live the commandments. When we live God's commandments, we live a holy life. We show that we belong to God. We are children of God.

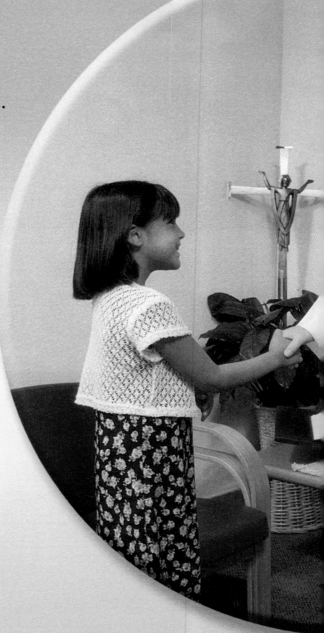

Jesus gave us the sacraments. The sacraments make us sharers in God's own life. We receive the grace to grow as children of God and live a holy life.

Penance is one of the sacraments. This sacrament is also called by other names. It is called the sacrament of Reconciliation. We can celebrate this sacrament together with other members of our church family and the priest. Or we can celebrate it individually with the priest.

We celebrate this sacrament for the first time before we receive First Communion. In this sacrament we are forgiven the sins that we commit after we are baptized. We sin when we freely choose to do what we know is against what God wants us to do. We also sin when we choose not to do something we know God wants us to do. Every sin hurts our friendship with God and with other people.

TOGETHER AS A FAMILY

Share responses to the question on this page. This week choose ways that your family members can better live the Great Commandment. For example: If family members hurt one another, show how much you truly care for one another. Talk about what happened and reconcile with one another.

Why do we celebrate Reconciliation?

What Difference Does This Make in My Life?

MY FAITH CHOICE

Talk with someone about one thing that you will do this week to live the Great Commandment.

Jesus gave us the sacrament of Reconciliation. When we celebrate this sacrament, we are made friends again with God and with one another. We receive the grace to live the Great Commandment.

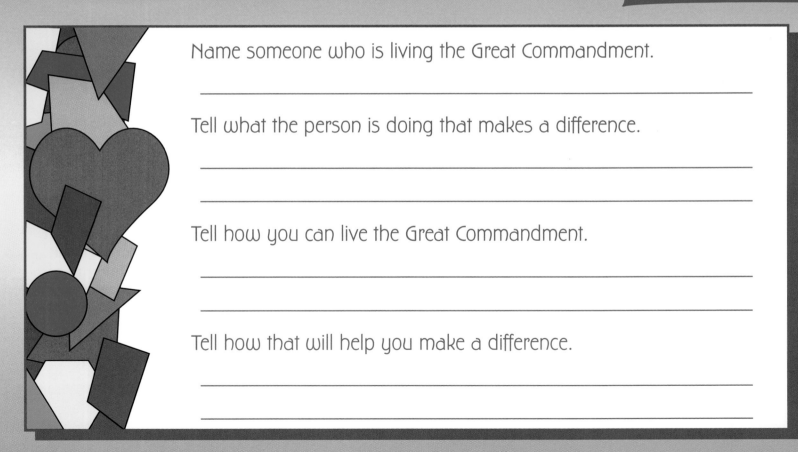

Name someone who is living the Great Commandment.

_____

Tell what the person is doing that makes a difference.

_____

_____

Tell how you can live the Great Commandment.

_____

_____

Tell how that will help you make a difference.

_____

_____

TOGETHER AS A FAMILY

Remembering Together

In this chapter your child learned about the Great Commandment. The Great Commandment teaches that we are to live a holy life. We are to love God with our whole heart and soul, and we are to love others as we love ourselves (see Matthew 22:34–40). In the sacrament of Reconciliation we receive God's forgiveness for our choosing not to live the Great Commandment. Talk with your child about living the Great Commandment. Use these or similar questions:

- How does our family help one another live the Great Commandment?
- Who are models for living the Great Commandment?
- How do we show we are sorry when we do not live the Great Commandment?
- How does our conscience help us to live the Great Commandment?

Sharing Together

Choose one of these activities to do together or design a similar activity of your own:

- Watch a favorite TV show together. Afterward discuss how the people in the show are living the Great Commandment.
- Have each family member write on an index card how your family can live the Great Commandment. Choose one thing that you will do together.

- Talk about ways your family can resolve to settle conflicts peacefully.

Visit the RCL sacraments web site by following the link titled "Sacraments" at www.FaithFirst.com.

Praying Together

Pray this or a similar prayer at family meals or at other family prayer times this week:

God, our loving Father,
you gave us the Great Commandment.
Send us the Holy Spirit
to help us live the Great Commandment every day.
We ask this through Jesus Christ our Lord. Amen.

Getting Ready Together

This is an appropriate time to briefly review the parts of the rites of Reconciliation with your child. Go through the rite of Reconciliation that your son or daughter will celebrate. "The Individual Rite for Reconciliation" and "The Communal Rite for Reconciliation" are found on pages 52–63 of this book.

CHAPTER 3

We Listen to the Holy Spirit

Holy Spirit,
help us to follow Jesus,
the Light of the World.

Sharing Together

In the opening prayer we lit a candle. We talked about how the Holy Spirit is always with us. What was it like for you to pray around the lighted candle?

When does your family use lighted candles?

As Catholics we use lighted candles to remind us that Jesus is the Light of the World. Give one example of when we use lighted candles in church.

_____

_____

_____

The Good Samaritan

At Baptism we are given a lighted candle. This reminds us to live as followers of Jesus, the Light of the World. Read this Bible story to discover how we can live as followers of Jesus.

Robbers attacked a man on a road. The robbers hurt the man and stole everything he had. Running away, they left the man lying on the ground. A traveler soon came down the road. He saw the injured man lying on the road. But he chose to walk by without helping him. A second traveler also saw the injured man and walked by.

Then a traveler from Samaria came down the road. This traveler stopped and took care of the injured man. After he bandaged the man's wounds, he put the man on his donkey and he brought the injured man to an inn. Arriving at the inn, the Samaritan said to the owner, "Take care of this injured man. I will pay you whatever it costs."

BASED ON LUKE 10:29–37

FAITH FOCUS

What does the Bible story of the good Samaritan teach us?

The traveler who helped the man is called the good Samaritan. What did the good Samaritan choose to do?

TOGETHER AS A FAMILY

Share responses to the question on this page. This week choose ways that your family members can be lights in the world. For example: Cook a meal together and bring it to a family who is caring for someone who is sick.

We Make Good Decisions

FAITH FOCUS

What does it mean to confess our sins in the sacrament of Reconciliation?

WHAT WE SEE AND HEAR

We confess our sins individually to the priest. We can confess our sins to the priest either face-to-face or kneeling behind a screen. The priest will never tell anyone what we confess to him.

As the Samaritan did, we need to make good decisions and put our decisions into action. When we put our good decisions into action, we show we are followers of Jesus, the Light of the World.

Here are some of the things we can do to learn to make good decisions.

- **Pray** to the Holy Spirit.
- **Listen** to the word of God. Listen to what Jesus teaches about the Great Commandment, the Ten Commandments, and the Beatitudes.
- **Learn** what our church family teaches about how we are to live as children of God.
- **Talk** with parents, teachers, and other adults about what to do. Ask their help.
- **Choose** what we know is the right thing to do and do it.

We do not always make good decisions. We sometimes choose to sin. We turn our hearts away from God. The Holy Spirit helps us to know what our sins are. In Reconciliation we confess, or tell, our sins to the priest. This is why it is sometimes called the sacrament of confession. It is important that we accept responsibility for what we say and what we do.

We must confess any mortal sin we commit. A mortal sin is a serious offense against God or other people. It separates us from God. We may also confess venial sins, or less serious sins. Venial sins hurt, but do not break, our relationship with God.

We show that living as a child of God is important to us when we celebrate the sacrament of Reconciliation. It shows we want to do our best to live as Jesus taught us. This is why it is sometimes called the sacrament of conversion.

How does the sacrament of Reconciliation help us to live as lights in the world?

TOGETHER AS A FAMILY

Share responses to the question on this page. This week set aside a time for family members to talk about things that they have done or said that have hurt other family members. Name what was done or said and apologize. Decide what can be done to make things better.

What Difference Does This Make in My Life?

The sacrament of Reconciliation brings God's love and forgiveness into our lives right now. The Holy Spirit helps us to make decisions to show our love for God and for others.

MY FAITH CHOICE

Talk with someone about one thing you will do this week that shows you are a good Samaritan.

The story of the good Samaritan helps us to make good decisions. Check the people you would ask to help you make good decisions.

_____ **Parents**

_____ **Grandparents**

_____ **Priest**

_____ **Teachers**

_____ Friends

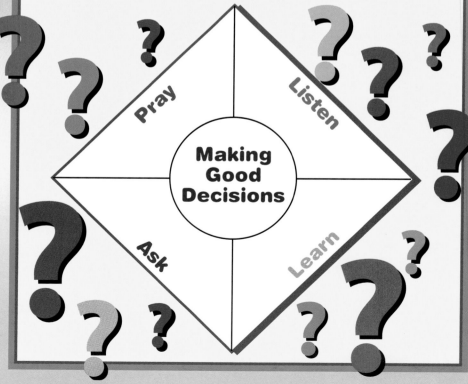

What helps you to make good decisions? Color the sections that name the things you will do.

Pray

Listen

Making Good Decisions

Ask

Learn

TOGETHER AS A FAMILY

Remembering Together

In this chapter your child learned that followers of Jesus are good Samaritans. They make good decisions that bring light to the world. Discuss responses to these or similar questions:

- How does our family help one another make good choices?
- How is our family a light in the world?
- How do we celebrate being lights in the world?

Sharing Together

Choose one of these activities to do together or design a similar activity of your own:

- Write a prayer together to the Holy Spirit, asking for help to make good decisions. Pray the prayer together this week.
- Light a candle during mealtime. Let the candle remind you that God has called you by name to be followers of Jesus, the Light of the World.
- Watch the television news together. Identify people who were good Samaritans. Choose one thing that your family can do to be good Samaritans.

 Visit the RCL sacraments web site by following the link titled "Sacraments" at www.FaithFirst.com.

Praying Together

Pray this or a similar prayer at family meals or at other family prayer times this week:

God, our loving Father,
today we gather to listen to the Holy Spirit.
We know that the Holy Spirit is always with us
to help us choose light over darkness.
We ask this through Jesus Christ our Lord. Amen.

Getting Ready Together

Review the "I confess" prayer on page 73. Then go through the "Confession of Sins" part of the rite of Reconciliation with your child. Discuss the difference between a mistake and a sin. Reassure your child that the priest will not tell anyone what he or she confesses in the sacrament of Reconciliation.

We Are Sorry

*God of mercy,
help us to seek forgiveness
and to forgive.*

Sharing Together

In the opening prayer we prayed the Our Father. What was it like for you to pray the Our Father together?

When do you pray with others?

As Catholics we ask God, our loving Father, for forgiveness. We forgive others as God forgives us when we are truly sorry. Give one example of how we show we are sorry.

_____

_____

_____

Zaccheus

Jesus taught us about being sorry. Read this Bible story to discover what Zaccheus did to show he was sorry.

Jesus came to a town called Jericho. A man named Zaccheus lived there. Zaccheus was a tax collector. He was a very wealthy man.

Zaccheus wanted to see Jesus. But the crowd was too large. So Zaccheus ran ahead and climbed a tree. When Jesus reached the tree, he saw Zaccheus and said, "Zaccheus, come down. I must stay at your house." Zaccheus was very happy. But many of the people were upset because Zaccheus had treated them unfairly.

Zaccheus said, "I will give people four times the money I unfairly took from them. I will also give half my money to the poor." Jesus said, "Today you have been saved."

BASED ON LUKE 19:1–10

FAITH FOCUS

What does the Bible story of Zaccheus teach us about being sorry?

Zacchaeus was unfair to people. What did Zacchaeus do to show he was sorry he hurt people?

TOGETHER AS A FAMILY

Share the Bible story about Zacchaeus. Discuss responses to the question on this page. Talk about the importance of what Zacchaeus said he would do.

We Tell God We Are Sorry

FAITH FOCUS

In Reconciliation how do we show we are truly sorry for our sins?

WHAT WE SEE AND HEAR

The priest usually wears a purple stole for the celebration of the sacrament of Reconciliation. The color purple is used as a sign of penance. The stole looks like a long scarf. It is worn by priests and bishops around their necks and over both shoulders.

Zacchaeus showed he was sorry for his sins. We too need to show we are sorry for our sins. Being sorry is a sign of love. It shows our love for God and for other people.

The Holy Spirit helps us to be sorry for our sins. The Holy Spirit helps us to turn to God and to other people and say, "I am sorry. I ask for your forgiveness."

The Holy Spirit also helps us to forgive others. When someone shows us they are sorry and says, "I am sorry. I ask for your forgiveness," the Holy Spirit helps us to forgive them. When we forgive others, we treat them the way God treats us. We are living as children of God.

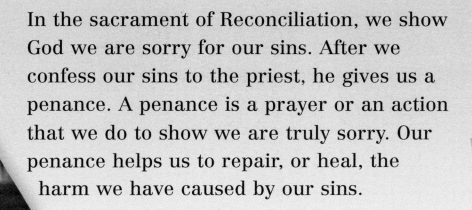

In the sacrament of Reconciliation, we show God we are sorry for our sins. After we confess our sins to the priest, he gives us a penance. A penance is a prayer or an action that we do to show we are truly sorry. Our penance helps us to repair, or heal, the harm we have caused by our sins.

After we accept our penance, we pray an act of contrition. An act of contrition is a prayer of sorrow. We tell God we are sorry for our sins with all our heart. We promise to do our penance and not to sin again. We promise to heal the harm we have caused by our sins. We ask God to help us avoid temptation. Temptation is whatever leads us to sin. We ask God's mercy in the name of Jesus.

How can we show that we are truly sorry for our sins?

What Difference Does This Make in My Life?

The Holy Spirit helps us to be sorry for our sins. In Reconciliation we show God we are sorry and ask for forgiveness. We receive the grace to forgive others as God forgives us.

MY FAITH CHOICE

Talk with someone about one thing that you can do or say this week to show you are sorry.

Look at the words and actions in the box. Circle the words or actions you would use to show you forgive someone.

"I am sorry."

Shake hands.

"It's your fault."

A pat on the back.

"That's okay."

A hug.

Write a story about a time when you said, "I am sorry." Use some of the words or actions you circled to help you write your story.

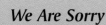

TOGETHER AS A FAMILY

Remembering Together

In this chapter your child learned about Zacchaeus and what it means to be sorry for our sins. Talk with your child about what he or she is learning. Share responses to these or similar questions:

- What did Jesus teach about being sorry for our sins?
- How do our family members show each other that we are truly sorry?
- How does our family share forgiveness with each other?
- How do we show that we have made up, or reconciled, with each other?

Sharing Together

Choose one of these activities to do together or design a similar activity of your own:

- Talk about the importance of family members being truly sorry and asking for and giving forgiveness when they offend each other. Retell a family story about forgiveness.
- Share ideas about ways your family can be forgiving. Choose one thing that you will do together.
- Write a prayer together to the Holy Spirit. Ask the Holy Spirit to help you be forgiving people. Pray the prayer together during the week.

- Make a centerpiece for the table. Write the words "Forgive and Seek Forgiveness" on the bottom half of an index card. Fold the index card in half and stand the centerpiece on your table to serve as a reminder for your family to be a forgiving people.

Visit the RCL sacraments web site by following the link titled "Sacraments" at www.FaithFirst.com.

Praying Together

Pray this or a similar prayer at family meals or at other family prayer times this week:

God, our loving Father,
today we gather to remember your great love for us.
Send us the Holy Spirit
to help us both forgive and seek forgiveness.
We ask this through Jesus Christ our Lord. Amen.

Getting Ready Together

Continue to review the parts of the rites of Reconciliation with your child. Take time to share ideas about the importance of accepting and doing our penance. Read the words of an act of contrition together. Talk about the meaning of the prayer. Help your child memorize the act of contrition that he or she will pray during the celebration of the sacrament.

CHAPTER 5

We Are Forgiven

*Loving God,
thank you for
your forgiving love.*

Sharing Together

In the opening prayer we placed our hands on each other's head. What was it like for you?

What do you do to make up, or reconcile, with others?

We share in God's forgiving love. We make up, or reconcile, with God and with others. Give one example of how we reconcile with God and with others.

_____

_____

_____

The Forgiving Father

Jesus told many stories about God's love for us. Here is one story Jesus told. Read the story to discover what the father does to show his love for his son.

A man had two sons. The younger son said to his father, "Father, give me my share of our family's money." So the father divided his money between his two sons. The younger son left home. He went off to live by himself. Soon the son wasted all his money. He had no money to buy food.

The son became very hungry. The son was very sorry and decided to return home. The father saw the son walking toward their home. He ran to his son and held him in his arms. The son said to his father, "Father, I am sorry." The father was very happy to have his son home again.

BASED ON LUKE 15:11–32

FAITH FOCUS

What does the Bible story tell us about God's love for us?

In the Bible story the father and his son make up. What do you think the story tells us about God's love for us?

TOGETHER AS A FAMILY

Share the Bible story about the forgiving father. Discuss responses to the question on this page. Talk about ways family members can reconcile, or make up, with one another.

The Gift of Forgiveness

FAITH FOCUS

In Reconciliation what is the sign of God's forgiving our sins?

WHAT WE SEE AND HEAR

In the sacrament of Reconciliation the priest extends his hand over our head as he prays the prayer of absolution. This gesture is used in the sacrament as a sign that the Holy Spirit is at work.

The Bible story of the forgiving father shows us how much God loves us. God always forgives us when we are truly sorry for our sins.

The sacraments make us sharers in God's mercy and forgiving love. In Baptism original sin and all sins we commit before Baptism are forgiven. When we celebrate the Eucharist, we share in God's forgiving love. All venial sins are forgiven and we receive the grace to avoid sin. Through the Eucharist we grow closer to God and to one another.

Sins committed after Baptism are forgiven in the sacrament of Reconciliation. Reconciliation is one of the Sacraments of Healing. In this sacrament the Holy Spirit reconciles us with God and with one another.

In the sacrament of Reconciliation Christ is present in the Church. Through the ministry of bishops and priests we are forgiven our sins. After we confess our sins, accept our penance, and tell God we are truly sorry, we receive absolution. *Absolution* means "pardon from sins."

The bishop or priest holds his hand over our head or places his hand on our head. He makes the sign of the cross over us as he prays,

> I absolve you from your sins
> in the name of the Father, and of the Son,
> and of the Holy Spirit.

We make the sign of the cross as the priest blesses us. Then we respond, "Amen."

In Reconciliation we are forgiven our sins. We are reconciled with God and with the Church. We look forward to living together with God, Jesus, Mary, and all the saints in heaven.

TOGETHER AS A FAMILY

Share responses to the question on this page. This week share words and actions that help to bring about reconciliation. For example, hug one another; use such expressions as "I love you," "I forgive you." When such things are said and done often, they more easily happen at those moments when reconciling with one another is needed.

How are our sins forgiven in Reconciliation?

What Difference Does This Make in My Life?

Forgiveness is a sign of love. It is a sign of God's love for us and of our love for other people. In the sacrament of Reconciliation we share in God's forgiving love. We are forgiven the sins we commit after Baptism. We receive the grace to forgive others.

MY FAITH CHOICE

Talk with someone about one thing you will do this week to be forgiving.

Think of a time when you forgave someone. Draw or write about what you did to show you forgave the person.

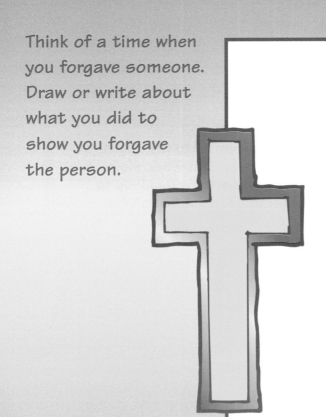

TOGETHER AS A FAMILY

Remembering Together

In this chapter your child listened to the story of the forgiving father. In the sacrament of Reconciliation God forgives us our sins. God shows us that he always loves us. Discuss responses to these or similar questions:

- How does our family help each other to be forgiving?
- How does our family show that we forgive each other?
- How does forgiveness help us share our love with each other?

Sharing Together

Sharing forgiveness shows our love for one another. Choose one of these activities to do together or design a similar activity of your own:

- Take turns sharing stories about times when you forgave each other. Talk about how these experiences helped you share your love with each other.
- Write a prayer together to the Holy Spirit asking for help to be forgiving. Pray the prayer together this week.
- Share ideas about ways your family can be like the forgiving father. Choose one thing that you will do together.

- Draw a picture of the forgiving father welcoming his son home. Post the picture where it can remind everyone to be forgiving.

 Visit the RCL sacraments web site by following the link titled "Sacraments" at www.FaithFirst.com.

Praying Together

Pray this or a similar prayer at family meals or at other prayer times this week:

God, our loving Father,
you send us the Holy Spirit.
Help us forgive one another as you forgive us.
We ask this through Jesus Christ our Lord. Amen.

Getting Ready Together

Continue to review the rite of Reconciliation with your child. In particular take time to read the words of absolution together. Have your child practice the response. Talk about the meaning of the prayer of absolution. The prayer of absolution is found on pages 55 and 61.

We Are Peacemakers

Holy Spirit,
help us to share the peace
of Christ with others.

Sharing Together

In the opening prayer we shared a sign of peace. What was it like for you?

How do you share peace with others?

As Catholics we are called to share the peace of Christ with one another. Give one example of how we share Christ's peace with others.

_____

_____

_____

The Gift of Peace

Jesus shared the gift of God's peace with us. Read this Bible story to discover one time when Jesus gave his followers the gift of peace.

Jesus said to his disciples, "Soon, I will return to my Father. But do not be afraid. You will not be alone. The Father will send you the Holy Spirit in my name. The Holy Spirit will be with you always. The Holy Spirit will remind you of everything I taught you. If you love me, you will keep my commandments."

Jesus continued, "Rejoice with me. I am going to the Father. I give you the gift of my peace."

After Jesus died, he was raised from the dead. He went to his disciples and said, "Peace be with you."

BASED ON JOHN 14:15–27 AND 20:21

FAITH FOCUS

What did Jesus give his followers before he returned to his Father?

Jesus gave his disciples the gift of peace. How can we share peace with others?

TOGETHER AS A FAMILY

Share the Bible story about Jesus giving his followers the gift of peace. Discuss responses to the question on this page. This week choose one way that your family can share the gift of peace with one another.

Blessed Are the Peacemakers

FAITH FOCUS

Why do we share
the gift of peace
with others?

**WHAT WE
SEE AND HEAR**

Blessings are one of the
ways the Church shows
that God always shares
his love with us. All our
blessings remind us that
God, who knows and
loves each of us by
name, is always with us.
This is the greatest
blessing we could have.

Jesus taught that we are to share the gift of peace with others. He said,

> "Blessed are the peacemakers.
> They are children of God."
> BASED ON MATTHEW 5:9

Jesus told his disciples they were to be peacemakers. Our Church teaches us that peacemakers act justly. This means that we love and treat people fairly. We are kind to people, even to people who are unkind to us. We respect all people. All people are children of God. God created people in his image and likeness.

We live as peacemakers when we forgive others and ask others to forgive us. The Holy Spirit gives us the courage to live as peacemakers. This is not always easy to do.

In the sacrament of Reconciliation, God forgives our sins and shares his gift of peace with us. We receive the grace of the Holy Spirit to share the gifts of forgiveness and peace with others.

At the end of the celebration of Reconciliation, the priest tells us,
> Go in peace,
> and proclaim to the world
> the wonderful works of God
> who has brought you forgiveness.

We respond, "Amen."

We are reconciled with God and with one another. We want everyone to know how wonderful God's love is. We choose to live as peacemakers. We are living signs of the kingdom of God where we will all live in peace with God, Jesus, Mary, and the saints forever.

What do we do to live as peacemakers?

TOGETHER AS A FAMILY

Share responses to the question on this page. Create a poster or banner with the words "Blessed are the peacemakers. They are children of God." Display the poster or banner in a place where your family can see it.

What Difference Does This Make in My Life?

We forgive others as God forgives us because we are children of God. We are kind to others as God is kind to us. We are merciful to others as God is merciful to us. We are peacemakers.

Jesus said, "Blessed are the peacemakers." Who do you know who is a peacemaker? What does that person do?

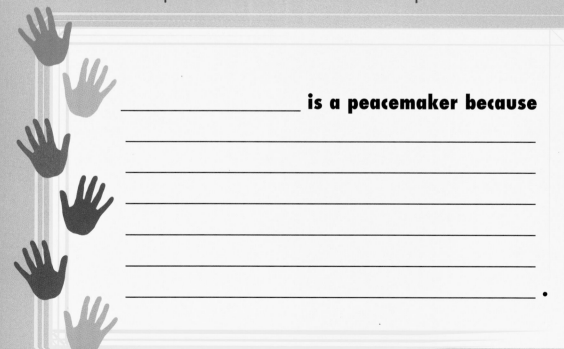

_____ is a peacemaker because

_____

_____

_____

_____

_____ .

MY FAITH CHOICE

Talk with someone about one thing that you will do this week to live as a peacemaker.

How can you be a peacemaker?

I can be a peacemaker by _____

_____

_____

_____

_____

_____ .

TOGETHER AS A FAMILY

Remembering Together

In this chapter your child listened to the Bible story of Jesus giving the disciples the gift of peace. We receive the gift of God's peace and give thanks to God for that gift in the sacrament of Reconciliation. Discuss responses to these or similar questions with your child:

- How does the Holy Spirit help our family live as peacemakers?
- How does our family share Jesus' gift of peace with each other?
- How does our family live as peacemakers in the world?

Sharing Together

Choose one of these activities to do together or design a similar activity of your own:

- Watch television together. When violence is shown, especially in cartoons, point out that violence is never funny. Talk about ways people can peacefully solve the conflicts shown.
- Make a symbol of the Holy Spirit, such as a dove or a flame. Display the symbol where it can remind everyone to live as peacemakers.

 Visit the RCL sacraments web site by following the link titled "Sacraments" at www.FaithFirst.com.

Praying Together

The Holy Spirit is our helper, teacher, and guide. This is an appropriate time to help your child learn this prayer. Make it a prayer your family prays each day as you begin the final preparation for your child to receive the sacrament of Reconciliation.

Come, Holy Spirit, fill the hearts of your faithful.
And kindle in them the fire of your love.
Send forth your Spirit and they shall be created.
And you will renew the face of the earth. Amen.

Getting Ready Together

Continue sharing the rite of Reconciliation with your child. In particular review the dismissal and thanksgiving rites, which are found on page 56 and pages 62 and 63 of this book. Have your child practice the responses. Talk about the meaning of the words. As you and your child make final preparations for his or her celebration of the sacrament of Reconciliation, go through the entire rite of Reconciliation that will be celebrated. Take the time to answer any questions your child may ask. Begin and end with a short prayer, for example, "God and Father of us all, you forgive our sins and send us your peace. Help us to forgive each other and to work together for peace in the world" (based on *Rite of Penance* 211).

Celebrating Reconciliation

Jesus gave us the sacraments. Christ is present in the Church and acting in the sacraments. The sacraments make us sharers in the life and love of God. They make us one with God and with our church family. We receive grace to live holy lives as children of God and followers of Jesus.

The sacrament of Reconciliation is one of the sacraments Jesus gave the Church. After he was raised from the dead, Jesus gave the apostles the gift of the Holy Spirit and the power to forgive sins (John 20:21–23). The Church does this work today through the power of the Holy Spirit and the ministry of bishops and priests. One important way they do this is in the sacrament of Reconciliation.

Here are two ways we can take part in the celebration of the sacrament of Reconciliation.

The Individual Rite for Reconciliation

Examination of Conscience

We prepare ourselves to celebrate this sacrament. Before we meet with the priest, we examine our conscience. We spend time praying. We ask the Holy Spirit to help us know how we have failed to live as children of God and followers of Jesus.

Examining our conscience helps us to name our sins and to tell God we are sorry. There is a list of questions on page 64 of this book that will help you examine your conscience.

GREETING

The priest greets us. Together, we pray the Sign of the Cross.

Priest and penitent: In the name of the Father, and of the Son, and of the Holy Spirit. Amen.

Next, the priest reminds us how much God loves us. The priest may pray, using these or similar words:

Priest: May God, who has enlightened every heart, help you to know your sins and trust in his mercy.

Penitent: Amen.

READING THE WORD OF GOD

The priest may read a story from the Bible to us or welcome us with words from the Bible. The Bible is the story of God's love and mercy. When we listen to the Bible, we are listening to God's own word to us. God is telling us that he always loves us. He is telling us what it means to be a child of God. Here is a story the priest might read to you.

A man had two sons. The younger son said to his father, "Father, give me my share of our family's money." So the father divided his money between his two sons. The younger son left home. He went off to live by himself. Soon the son wasted all his money. He had no money to buy food.

The son became very hungry. The son was very sorry and decided to return home. The father saw the son walking toward their home. He ran to his son and held him in his arms. The son said to his father, "Father, I am sorry." The father was very happy to have his son home again.

BASED ON LUKE 15:11–32

CONFESSION OF SINS AND ACCEPTANCE OF A PENANCE

Confession of Sins

We tell our sins to the priest. The priest will never tell anyone the sins we confess to him. When we confess our sins, we show that we trust that God always loves us. We show we care about our friendship with God. We must confess mortal sins. We may also confess venial sins.

Acceptance of Our Penance

After we confess our sins, the priest talks to us. He names some of the ways we can live a holy life. He gives us a penance. A penance is something we do or say that shows we are sorry for and want to make up for our sins. Our penance helps us to repair or heal the harm we have caused by our sins. We accept and promise to do the penance. We say or do our penance as soon as possible after celebrating the sacrament. When we are truly sorry for our sins, we want to make up, or be reconciled, with God and with the Church. We want to live as Jesus taught us.

PRAYER OF SORROW AND ABSOLUTION

Prayer of Sorrow

We pray a prayer of sorrow. Our prayer of sorrow is called an act of contrition. This shows we are truly sorry for our sins. We can pray this form of the act of contrition or we can pray one of the other prayers of sorrow the Church gives us (see "My Daily Prayers," page 71). Or we can also use our own words.

My God,
I am sorry for my sins
with all my heart.
In choosing to do wrong
and failing to do good,
I have sinned against you
whom I should love above all things.
I firmly intend, with your help,
to do penance,
to sin no more,
and to avoid whatever leads me to sin.
Our Savior Jesus Christ
suffered and died for us.
In his name, my God, have mercy.

Absolution

Jesus gave the apostles the ministry, or work, to forgive sins. Bishops and priests share in that same work. God forgives us our sins through the words and actions of the priest in the sacrament of Reconciliation. The priest extends his hands over our head or places his hands on our head as he prays:

Priest: God, the Father of mercies,
through the death and
resurrection of his Son
has reconciled the world
to himself
and sent the Holy Spirit
among us
for the forgiveness of sins;
through the ministry
of the Church
may God give you pardon
and peace,

The priest makes the sign of the cross over our head as he says:

and I absolve you from your sins
in the name of the Father,
and of the Son, †
and of the Holy Spirit.

We may make the sign of the cross as the priest blesses us. Then we respond,

Penitent: Amen.

Our Amen shows that we believe that God has forgiven our sins. We are made one again, or reconciled, with God and with our church family.

PRAISE OF GOD AND DISMISSAL

Praise of God

God forgives us as the father in the Bible story forgave his younger son. Together with the priest we praise God.

Priest: Give thanks to the Lord, for he is good.

Penitent: His mercy endures for ever.

Dismissal

The priest sends us forth. He says these or similar words:

Priest: Go in peace, and proclaim to the world the wonderful works of God who has brought you salvation.

We are children of God. We want to tell everyone about God's love. We share God's gift of peace with our family, friends, and neighbors. We are peacemakers.

The Communal Rite for Reconciliation

We can celebrate this sacrament with other members of our church family. Together we listen to the word of God. We listen to the story of God's love for us. We are invited to conversion, or to live as Jesus taught us. We examine our conscience. We take a careful look at how we are living as children of God and followers of Jesus. We help each other through prayer.

INTRODUCTORY RITES

Song

We gather as the community of the Church. As the priests, readers, and other ministers enter, we stand. We sing a hymn about forgiveness or peace. We remember how much God loves us.

> **All:** Hear us, Lord,
> for you are merciful and kind.
> In your great compassion,
> look on us with love.

Greeting

The priest greets us. His words remind us that the Holy Spirit and God's grace invite us to be sorry for our sins and to celebrate this sacrament. He welcomes us with these or similar words:

> **Priest:** Grace, mercy, and peace
> be with you from God the Father
> and Christ Jesus our Savior.
>
> **All:** And also with you.

Opening Prayer

The priest invites us to pray. He uses these or similar words:

Priest: Brothers and sisters, God calls us to conversion; let us therefore ask him for the grace of sincere repentance.

We pray in silence for a few minutes. Then the priest prays aloud.

Priest: Lord,
hear the prayers of those
who call on you,
forgive the sins of those
who confess to you,
and in your merciful love
give us your pardon and
your peace.
We ask this through Christ
our Lord.

All: Amen.

CELEBRATION OF THE WORD OF GOD

We listen attentively to the Bible, the word of God. There may be several readings. There is always a reading from the Gospel. As we listen to the readings, the Holy Spirit invites us to think about God's love and mercy and to be sorry for our sins.

First Reading

We sit and listen to a story about God's love and mercy from the Old Testament. The reader concludes, saying,

Reader: The word of the Lord.

All: Thanks be to God.

Psalm Response

We show that we trust God and his love and mercy by singing or saying several verses of a psalm. For example:

Reader: All my hope, O Lord, is in your loving kindness.

All: All my hope, O Lord, is in your loving kindness.

Second Reading

We remain seated and listen again as God tells us about his love and mercy. This reading is from the New Testament, but not from the Gospels. The reader concludes, saying,

Reader: The word of the Lord.

All: Thanks be to God.

Alleluia or Gospel Acclamation

Jesus is present with us. We stand and greet Jesus, who speaks to us in the Gospel. For example, we sing or say,

All: Alleluia.

Gospel

Jesus tells us about God's mercy and love for us. He shows us the way to live as children of God and peacemakers. The priest begins,

Priest: A reading from the holy gospel according to (name of Gospel writer).

The priest concludes by saying,

Priest: The gospel of the Lord.

All: Praise to you, Lord Jesus Christ.

Homily

The priest helps us to think about what God's word is saying to us.

Examination of Conscience

We think about how we are living as children of God. We ask the Holy Spirit to help us to be sorry for our sins and to give us the courage to live as Jesus taught us.

RITE OF RECONCILIATION

Expressing Our Sorrow Together

Together, as God's people, we respond to the Holy Spirit. We express our sorrow for our sins to God and one another. We use these or similar words:

All: I confess to almighty God,
         and to you, my brothers
            and sisters,
         that I have sinned through
            my own fault
         in my thoughts and in my words,
         in what I have done,
         and in what I have failed to do;
         and I ask blessed Mary,
            ever virgin,
         all the angels and saints,
         and you, my brothers and sisters,
         to pray for me to the Lord
            our God.

Next, we stand and pray a litany of contrition or sing a song. Then we pray the Lord's Prayer. Jesus often told us about his love for his Father and God the Father's love for us. In this prayer, we call God "Father" as Jesus invited us to do. We tell God the Father how much we love him. We ask him for the grace we need to live as children of God.

Priest: Let us now pray to God
            our Father in the words
            Christ gave us, and ask
            him for his forgiveness
            and protection from
            all evil.

All: Our Father . . .

Individual Confession and Absolution

We then go individually to the priest to confess our sins. The priest gives us a penance. We say or do our penance as soon as possible after celebrating the sacrament. Doing the penance is a sign that we want to change our lives. We want to repair, or heal, the harm we have caused by our sins. Then the priest, in the name of God, absolves us, or frees us, from our sins. The priest extends his hands over our head or places his hands on our head as he prays:

Priest: God, the Father of mercies,
through the death and
resurrection of his Son
has reconciled the world
to himself
and sent the Holy Spirit
among us
for the forgiveness of sins;
through the ministry
of the Church
may God give you pardon
and peace,

He makes the sign of the cross over our head as he says:

and I absolve you
from your sins
in the name of the Father,
and of the Son, †
and of the Holy Spirit.

We may make the sign of the cross as the priest blesses us. Then we respond,

Penitent: Amen.

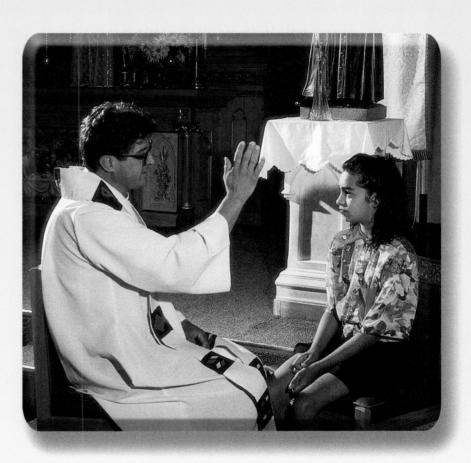

Proclamation of Praise
for God's Mercy

We have been reconciled with God and with our church family. Our friendship with God and one another has been made stronger. We sing a psalm or hymn or say a litany praising God for his mercy. For example:

Reader: The Lord is loving and kind:
his mercy is for ever.

All: The Lord is loving and kind:
his mercy is for ever.

Reader: Worship the Lord with
gladness;
come to his presence with
singing.

All: The Lord is loving and kind:
his mercy is for ever.

Reader: Know that the Lord is God.
It is he that made us, and
we are his.

All: The Lord is loving and kind:
his mercy is for ever.

PSALM 100:2–3

Concluding Prayer of Thanksgiving

Together, we give thanks to God. The priest leads us in prayer, using these or similar words:

Priest: All-holy Father,
you have shown us
your mercy
and made us a new creation
in the likeness of your Son.
Make us living signs of
your love
for the whole world to see.
We ask this through Christ
our Lord.

All: Amen.

CONCLUDING RITE

Blessing and Dismissal

The sacrament of Reconciliation has changed us. God has given us the grace of his forgiveness. He has strengthened our friendship with him and with one another. Before we leave, the priest asks God to bless us. He asks God to give us the grace to live as children of God.

Priest: May the Lord guide your
hearts in the way of his love
and fill you with Christ-like
patience.

All: Amen.

Priest: May he give you strength
to walk in newness of life
and to please him in all things.

All: Amen.

Priest: May almighty God bless you,
the Father,
and the Son †
and the Holy Spirit.

All: Amen.

The priest sends us forth. He says these or similar words:

Priest: The Lord has freed you
from your sins.
Go in peace.

All: Thanks be to God.

We are children of God. We want to tell everyone about God's love. We share God's gift of peace with our family, friends, and neighbors. We are peacemakers.

Song

We may sing a closing song praising and thanking God for his gift of forgiveness.

Examination of Conscience

We examine our conscience to help us live as children of God and followers of Jesus. We ask ourselves how well we are living or not living as Jesus taught us. We think about the Ten Commandments, the Beatitudes, and what the Church teaches us. We can ask ourselves questions like these:

■ How am I showing or failing to show my love and respect for God?

—Do I spend time with God in prayer? Do I listen reverently to God's word at Mass?

—Do I speak God's name or Jesus' name respectfully? Or have I spoken God's name or Jesus' name inappropriately when I was angry or to impress my friends?

■ How am I showing or failing to show my love and respect for other people and for myself?

—Do I respect my parents, teachers, and others who have the responsibility to care for me? Do I cooperate with them and obey them?

—Do I care for my health and follow safety rules?

—Do I treat other people fairly and with kindness? Or have I been mean to others?

—Am I generous? Do I share what I have with others, especially people in need? Or have I been greedy?

—Am I truthful? Or have I lied to get out of trouble or to get someone else into trouble?

The Ten Commandments

Jesus said that he did not come to do away with the commandments. He said he came to tell us their true meaning. The Ten Commandments guide us in living the Great Commandment: "Love the Lord your God with all your heart. Love your neighbor as you love yourself" (Matthew 22:37–40).

The First, Second, and Third Commandments tell us ways that we are to show our love and respect for God.

The Fourth through Tenth Commandments tell us ways that we are to show our love and respect for other people and for ourselves.

First Commandment: **I am the LORD your God: you shall not have strange gods before me.** There is only one God. Love God above all else. Keep God first in your life. Pray to God regularly. Honor God by living as a child of God.

Second Commandment: **You shall not take the name of the LORD your God in vain.** Speak the name of God, of Jesus, and of Mary with respect. Treat all holy things with respect.

Third Commandment: **Remember to keep holy the LORD's Day.** Remember and thank God for all the wonderful things he has done. Keep God at the center of the day—not work, shopping, or anything else. Worship God on Sundays and on holy days with your church family. Pray often, for example, at mealtimes, at bedtime, when you wake up, and during the day.

Fourth Commandment: Honor your father and your mother.
Honor your parents, grandparents, teachers, and leaders of your community and country. Respect and obey your parents and those who have the responsibility to care for you.

Fifth Commandment: You shall not kill.
Respect all life as a holy gift from God. Take care of your health. Take care of your mind and body. Care for people and all God's creation.

Sixth Commandment: You shall not commit adultery.
Be faithful to the members of your family and your friends. Keep your promises to do good. Respect your body and the bodies of others.

Seventh Commandment: You shall not steal.
Be honest. Ask permission to use what belongs to other people and take care of it. Return it when you are finished using it.

Eighth Commandment: You shall not bear false witness against your neighbor.
Be honest. Tell the truth.

Ninth Commandment: You shall not covet your neighbor's wife.
Respect the family and friends of other people. Do and say things that help good friends become better friends.

Tenth Commandment: You shall not covet your neighbor's goods.
Thank God for your blessings. Share what you have with others, especially people in need. See the blessings that other people have as a reminder of how wonderful and good God is.

The Beatitudes

God made everyone to be happy with him and with everyone else. God wants us to be happy now and forever in heaven. Jesus taught us that there are certain choices we can make that can bring us and other people happiness. These choices are called the Beatitudes. Living the Beatitudes helps us to discover the happiness that God wants us and all people to have.

Blessed are the poor in spirit,
for theirs is the kingdom of heaven.
Happy are people who have faith in God and trust in his love for them.

Blessed are those who mourn,
for they will be comforted.
Happy are people who become sad when they see people suffering and do what they can to help.

Blessed are the meek,
for they will inherit the earth.
Happy are people who are kind to others and treat them with respect.

Blessed are they who hunger and thirst for righteousness, for they will be filled.
Happy are people who treat other people fairly.

Blessed are the merciful,
for they will receive mercy.
Happy are people who forgive others as
God forgives them.

Blessed are the pure in heart,
for they will see God.
Happy are people who keep God first in
their lives and let nothing take the place
of God in their hearts.

Blessed are the peacemakers,
for they will be called children of God.
Happy are people who solve problems
without hurting anyone. They treat all
people with kindness and help others to
do the same.

Blessed are those who are
persecuted for righteousness' sake,
for theirs is the kingdom of heaven.
Happy are people who do what God wants,
even when people laugh at them or say
they will hurt them.

The Precepts of the Church

The Holy Spirit helps the Church to teach us how to live as children of God. One way that the Church does this is by making laws that help us live the Gospel. The precepts of the Church are a special kind of law. They tell us what Catholics must do to show our love for God and for other people. They help us to live the commandments and the Beatitudes. The precepts of the Church are:

- Take part in Mass on Sundays and on holy days of obligation.

- Confess our sins to a priest at least once a year if we have committed a serious, or mortal, sin.

- Receive Holy Communion at least once a year during the fifty days of the Easter season.

- Keep holy Sunday and the holy days of obligation.

- Fast and abstain on the days named by the Church.

- Share our possessions and talents with our church family to help the Church share the good news of Jesus with others.

My Daily Prayers

Sign of the Cross

In the name of the Father,
and of the Son,
and of the Holy Spirit. Amen.

Glory Prayer

Glory to the Father,
    and to the Son,
    and to the Holy Spirit:
as it was in the beginning, is now,
    and will be for ever. Amen.

Lord's Prayer

Our Father, who art in heaven,
hallowed be thy name;
thy kingdom come;
thy will be done on earth
    as it is in heaven.
Give us this day our daily bread;
and forgive us our trespasses
as we forgive those who trespass
    against us;
and lead us not into temptation,
but deliver us from evil. Amen.

Hail Mary

Hail Mary, full of grace,
the Lord is with you!
Blessed are you among women,
and blessed is the fruit
    of your womb, Jesus.
Holy Mary, Mother of God,
pray for us sinners,
now and at the hour of our death. Amen.

Grace before Meals

Bless us, O Lord,
    and these your gifts
which we are about to receive
    from your goodness.
Through Christ our Lord.
Amen.

Grace after Meals

We give you thanks for all your gifts,
    almighty God,
living and reigning now and for ever.
Amen.

Morning Prayer

Dear God,
as I begin this day,
keep me in your love and care.
Help me to live as your child today.
Bless me, my family, and my friends
    in all we do.
Keep us all close to you. Amen.

Evening Prayer

Dear God,
I thank you for today.
Keep me safe throughout the night.
Thank you for all the good I did today.
I am sorry for what I have chosen
    to do wrong.
Bless my family and friends. Amen.

Act of Contrition

My God,
I am sorry for my sins
with all my heart.
In choosing to do wrong
and failing to do good,
I have sinned against you
whom I should love above all things.
I firmly intend, with your help,
to do penance,
to sin no more,
and to avoid whatever leads me to sin.
Our Savior Jesus Christ
suffered and died for us.
In his name, my God, have mercy.

I Confess (Confiteor)

I confess to almighty God,
and to you, my brothers and sisters,
that I have sinned through my own fault
in my thoughts and in my words,
in what I have done,
and in what I have failed to do;
and I ask blessed Mary, ever virgin,
all the angels and saints,
and you, my brothers and sisters,
to pray for me to the Lord our God.

Prayer of Sorrow

Father,
I am sorry for all my sins:
for what I have done,
and for what I have failed to do.
I will sincerely try to do better.
I will especially try to (tell God
something that you will try to do better).
Help me walk by your light.

(Appendix II, *Rite of Penance* 51)

Prayer to the Holy Spirit

Come, Holy Spirit,
fill our hearts
with the fire of your love.

Prayer of Blessing and Adoration

We worship you, O God.
You are our God.
We are the sheep of your flock.

BASED ON PSALM 95:6–7

Prayer of Petition

Hear my prayer, O God,
for you are good and forgiving.

BASED ON PSALM 86:1, 5

Prayer of Intercession

Lord God, show your favor
to your people.

BASED ON PSALM 106:4

Prayer of Praise

Praise God,
for he is good.
His love lasts forever.

BASED ON PSALM 106:1

Prayer of Thanksgiving

Thank you, God,
for you are good.
You will always love me.

BASED ON PSALM 107:1

Glossary

A

absolution

Absolution is the priest's prayer for the forgiveness of our sins that we receive from God through the Church in the sacrament of Reconciliation.

absolve

The word *absolve* means "to take away." We are absolved from our sins in the sacrament of Reconciliation.

act of contrition

An act of contrition is a prayer of sorrow for our sins. The word *contrition* means "being sorry."

actual grace

Actual grace is the grace given to us by the Holy Spirit to help us live a holy life.

B

Baptism

Baptism is one of the Sacraments of Initiation. In Baptism we are joined to Christ. We share in Jesus' death and resurrection. God shares his life with us. We become adopted sons and daughters of God. We become members of the Church and followers of Jesus. Our sins are forgiven. We receive the gift of the Holy Spirit.

Beatitudes

The Beatitudes are sayings or teachings of Jesus. They name the actions of people that lead to the happiness God wants us to have now and forever. The word *beatitude* means "blessing" or "happiness."

Bible

The Bible is the written word of God. The Holy Spirit inspired, or guided, the people of God to write the Bible. The Old Testament and the New Testament are the two main parts of the Bible. The Bible is also called the Sacred Scriptures.

C–D

Church

The Church is the community of people who belong to Jesus Christ. The Church is the People of God, the Body of Christ, and the temple of the Holy Spirit.

confess

The word *confess* means "to admit that one has done something wrong." In the sacrament of Reconciliation we confess, or tell, our sins to the priest. Another name for the sacrament of Reconciliation is the sacrament of confession.

conscience

Conscience is a gift from God that helps us to know what is right and what is wrong.

conversion

Conversion is turning away from sin and living as a child of God. We receive God's help to do this in the sacrament of Reconciliation. This is why this sacrament is also called the sacrament of conversion.

decision

A decision is a choice made after careful thought.

E–F–G

Eucharist

The Eucharist is one of the Sacraments of Initiation. The Eucharist is the sacrament of the real presence of Jesus under the appearances of bread and wine. The Eucharist is the sacrament in which we receive the Body and Blood of Christ. The Eucharist makes present the sacrifice Jesus freely offered for the forgiveness of sins.

examination of conscience

The word *examine* means "to look at carefully." In our examination of conscience we ask the Holy Spirit to help us take a careful look at how we are living as children of God.

free will

Free will is the gift from God that helps us to choose between good and evil.

grace

The word *grace* means "gift." Grace is the gift of God's life and love the Holy Spirit shares with us. God's grace helps us to live as children of God and followers of Jesus.

Great Commandment

The Great Commandment is the commandment that all God's laws depend on. There are two parts that make up the Great Commandment. The first part tells us that we are to love God with our whole heart, mind, and soul. The second part tells us that we are to love others as we love ourselves.

H–I–J

heaven

Heaven is being happy with God, Jesus, Mary, and all the saints forever after our life on earth has ended.

hell

Hell is living separated from God forever after we die.

holiness

Holiness is a gift, or grace, from God. It is the gift of sharing in God's life and love and living as a child of God.

Holy Spirit

The Holy Spirit is the third Person of the Holy Trinity.

Holy Trinity

The Holy Trinity is a name for God. It tells us what God has told us about himself. There is one God in three Persons—God the Father, God the Son, and God the Holy Spirit.

Jesus Christ

Jesus Christ is the Son of God, the second Person of the Holy Trinity who became one of us. Jesus is true God and true man. By his death and resurrection Jesus saved us from our sins and reconciled us to God and to one another.

K–L–M–N

kingdom of God

The kingdom of God is the time when people will live in peace and justice with God, one another, and all of God's creation.

mercy

Mercy is the love and kindness of God that is greater than we can ever expect to receive.

mortal sin

A mortal sin is a serious failure in our love and respect for God, ourselves, and others. For a sin to be mortal three things are necessary. (1) What we are choosing to do or not to do must be very seriously wrong. (2) We must know that what we are choosing to do or not to do is seriously wrong. (3) We must freely choose to do what we know is seriously wrong. A mortal sin is so serious that we separate ourselves from God by committing a mortal sin. A penitent must confess to the priest in the sacrament of Reconciliation any mortal sins he or she has committed.

O–P–Q

original sin

Original sin is the sin of the first humans that is passed on to us as their descendants. All humans lost the gift of holiness because of original sin.

peace

Peace is living in friendship with God and others.

Penance

The sacrament of Reconciliation is also called the sacrament of Penance.

penance

A penance is a prayer or a good deed we do that shows we are sorry for our sins and want to make better choices. In the sacrament of Reconciliation the priest gives us a penance to do or say. Our penance helps us to repair or heal the harm we have caused by our sins.

penitent

The penitent is the baptized person who takes part in the sacrament of Reconciliation. The word *penitent* means "one who is sorry for their sins."

R

Reconciliation

Reconciliation is one of the seven sacraments that Jesus gave us. In this sacrament God forgives us the sins we commit after Baptism. We are reconciled with God and with others in the Church.

reconciliation

The word *reconciliation* means "becoming friends again."

Resurrection

The Resurrection is God's raising Jesus from the dead to new and glorious life by the power of the Holy Spirit.

reverence

Reverence is the gift of the Holy Spirit that enables us to show honor and respect to God, people, and all creation.

S

sacramentals

Sacramentals are objects and blessings that we use in worship and prayer. Sacramentals help us to remember that God is always with us. They help us to grow closer to God the Father, Jesus, and the Holy Spirit.

sacraments

The sacraments are the seven special celebrations of the Church that Jesus gave us. They are Baptism, Confirmation, Eucharist, Reconciliation, Anointing of the Sick, Holy Orders, and Matrimony. Jesus is present with the Church in a special way in the sacraments. Celebrating the sacraments makes us sharers in God's life and love.

Sacred Scriptures

The Sacred Scriptures are the written word of God. The Sacred Scriptures are also called the Bible.

sanctifying grace

Sanctifying grace is the gift of God's life and love. We receive sanctifying grace at Baptism. It makes us holy. Mortal sin takes away sanctifying grace. If we commit mortal sin, God gives us the gift of sanctifying grace again through the sacrament of Reconciliation.

Savior

Savior is a name we give to Jesus. Jesus saved us from our sins and reconciled us to God and to one another.

sin

Sin is freely choosing to say or do something that we know is against God's laws. Sin is also freely choosing not to say or do something that we know is right. Sin always harms our relationship with God and with our church family.

sorrow

Sorrow is the sadness we feel because of our sins and the desire to make up with those we have hurt by our sins.

T–U

temptation

Temptation is something that tries to lead us to do or say what is against God's commandments.

Ten Commandments

The Ten Commandments are the laws made known by God to Moses and God's people. The Ten Commandments guide us in living as children of God. They help us to love God, others, and ourselves.

V–Z

venial sin

Venial sin weakens but does not break our friendship with God and our church family. Venial sin is less serious than mortal sin.

Zacchaeus

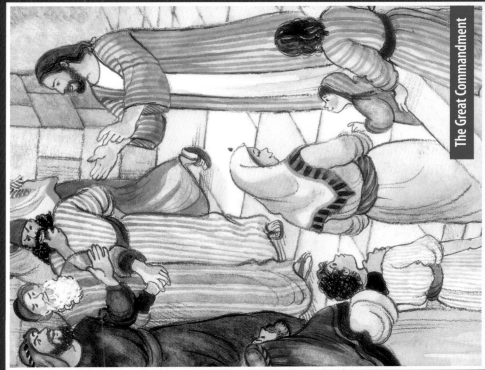

The Great Commandment

The Good Samaritan

God Loves Us

"Love others as much as you love yourself."

Based on Matthew 22:39

"Today you have been saved."

Based on Luke 19:9

"I have found my lost sheep."

Based on Luke 15:6

This traveler stopped and took care of the injured man.

Based on Luke 10:33

The Gift of Peace

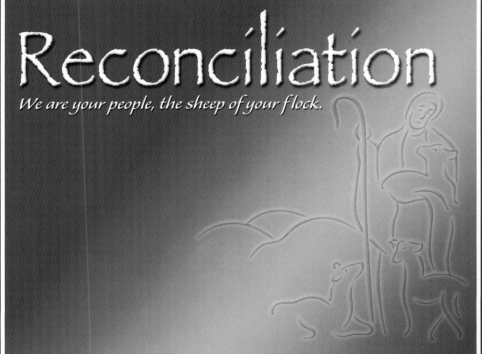

Reconciliation

We are your people, the sheep of your flock.

The Forgiving Father

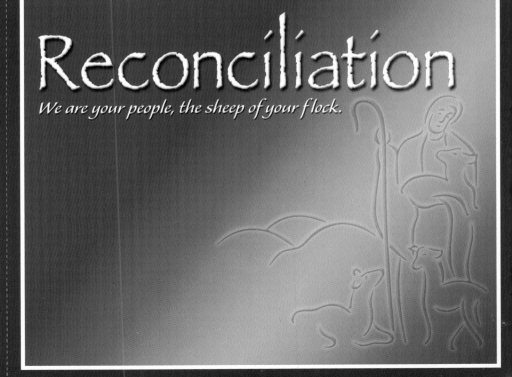

Reconciliation

We are your people, the sheep of your flock.

200 East Bethany Drive
Allen, TX 75002

"Peace be with you."

Based on John 20:21

200 East Bethany Drive
Allen, TX 75002

"Father, I am sorry."

Based on Luke 15:21

Reconciliation

_____

**has shared in God's loving forgiveness and mercy
by celebrating for the first time the Sacrament of Reconciliation**

at _____

(name of parish)

on _____

(date)

_____   _____

Pastor   *Catechist*

#2C451